Breaking the Silence:

Exposing the Truths Behind the Hoe Phase

BLK Diamond

ISBN: 978-2-6916-9191-0

First Edition

[Publisher's contact information, website, or social media handles can be included here.]

Published by BLK Diamond

Orlando, Florida

2023

Contents

Dedication

To all my haters,

You doubted my dreams, questioned my abilities, and attempted to bring me down. Your criticism and negativity only fueled my determination to rise above the noise.

I dedicate this book to you, for without your doubt, I wouldn't have discovered my strength. Your resistance became the catalyst for my resilience, and your negativity ignited my passion to prove you wrong.

Through every challenge and setback, I found the courage to persist, and in the face of your disbelief, I found the will to succeed.

Thank you for being the driving force behind my determination. Your doubts have only made me stronger, and your hatred has fueled my desire to shine.

With gratitude,

[Luis M Matta Jr] AKA BLK Diamond

Chapter 1
The Hookup Culture: A Comprehensive Overview

Casual sex and the hookup culture have become increasingly popular in today's modern society, where traditional relationship conventions are continuously altering. The purpose of this chapter is to present a detailed overview of hookup culture, its roots, and its impact on relationships and individual well-being.

To really comprehend the hookup culture, we must first investigate its origins. While casual sexual encounters are believed to have persisted throughout history, a substantial shift began to occur in the twentieth century. Social and cultural upheavals in the 1960s fuelled the sexual revolution, which challenged preconceived notions about relationships and sexuality. It cleared the way for a more accepting and open attitude toward casual sex.

The emphasis on pleasure and physical fulfillment is a crucial component of hookup culture. Participants engage in these meetings purely for sexual fulfillment, with no emotional attachment or commitment required. Individuals can explore their sexuality and experiment with different partners because of this deviation from traditional relationship rules. It provides a certain sense of freedom and emancipation, allowing people to prioritize their own desires and enjoyment.

Hookup culture, however, is not without its detractors. Some say that it encourages an objectification culture in which people are reduced to simply sexual objects. The emphasis on physical attractiveness and the fleeting nature of these meetings contribute to this view.

Critics are concerned that the hookup culture hampers the establishment of meaningful partnerships based on emotional closeness and connection.

Furthermore, the hookup culture has the potential to negatively damage individual well-being. Casual sexual encounters can elicit a range of emotions, both happy and negative. It creates a sense of empowerment and release for individuals, boosting self-confidence and self-esteem. Others, on the other hand, may feel remorse, guilt, or emotional emptiness after participating in casual sex. These opposing sentiments show the intricate psychological processes at work in hookup culture.

Plus, the hookup culture's ubiquity has generated worries about the possible consequences it entails, particularly to sexual health. Engaging in unprotected intercourse can raise the risk of sexually transmitted diseases (STIs) and unwanted pregnancies. Individuals must prioritize their sexual health and engage in safe sex behaviors such as using condoms and receiving STI testing on a regular basis.

As the first part of the chapter comes to a close, it is evident that hookup culture is a complicated phenomena with both positive and negative consequences. It undermines established relationship conventions by allowing people to explore their sexuality, but it also raises concerns about the influence on emotional well-being and the hazards involved.

We shall explore more into the impact of technology and societal variables on hookup culture in the second half of this chapter. Stay tuned for additional information on this fascinating subject.

The impact of technology and societal factors on hookup culture cannot be overstated. Dating apps and websites have transformed the way people interact and engage in casual sexual encounters in today's digital age. These platforms make it easier than ever to locate a casual hookup by providing a handy and accessible outlet for users to meet possible partners.

Tinder, Bumble, and Grindr are among the most popular dating applications among people looking for casual sexual interactions. Before meeting in person, users can look through profiles, swipe right for possible matches, and participate in conversation. The anonymity and convenience of these platforms have substantially aided the spread of hookup culture.

The introduction of technology and dating apps, on the other hand, has generated worries about the superficiality and objectification that can occur in hookup culture. Individuals are reduced to a simple snapshot with the sweep of a finger, judged purely on their outward appearance. The emphasis on rapid satisfaction and the plethora of options might foster a disposable mentality in which people are readily discarded and replaced.

Furthermore, social media platforms play an important part in promoting hookup culture. Sexualized content, such as provocative photographs and explicit dialogues, is becoming more widespread. These internet forums reinforce the validity and attractiveness of casual sex, driving its appeal among young adults.

Societal considerations also play a role in the normalizing of hookup culture. Gender roles are changing, there is a greater emphasis on personal independence and autonomy, and marriage is being delayed. Cultural standards and expectations have changed, allowing for a more permissive attitude toward casual sex.

However, it is critical to recognize that the hookup culture is not universally accepted. Traditional values and religious beliefs continue to impact people's attitudes on casual sex, frequently opposing the sexual liberation promoted by the hookup culture. Conflict and moral judgments might result from the clash of conservative ideals and the prevalent hookup culture.

Plus, the hookup culture can have serious consequences for one's emotional well-being. While some people thrive on casual sexual interactions, others may suffer psychological consequences. When traditional partnerships provide emotional connection, intimacy, and long-term commitment, feelings of loneliness, emptiness, and disappointment can occur.

In terms of sexual health, the hookup culture poses significant hazards. Casual intercourse without protection can expose people to sexually transmitted diseases (STIs) and unwanted pregnancies. Individuals must prioritize their sexual health and take essential precautions, such as wearing condoms and communicating openly about sexual boundaries and expectations.

As we near the end of this detailed examination of hookup culture, it becomes clear that it is a complex phenomena with numerous ramifications. While it promotes sexual exploration and liberation, it also raises concerns about emotional well-being, societal values, and sexual health. Individuals must negotiate the hookup culture intelligently, taking into account their own interests, boundaries, and the potential implications of their behavior.

By breaking the silence on the reality behind hookup culture, we can gain a better understanding of its influence on relationships and individual well-being. We can shed light on this prominent characteristic of modern society by investigating its origins, societal influences, and psychological dynamics.

In future chapters, we will delve further into the experiences and perspectives of individuals within the hookup culture. We will explore topics such as consent, communication, and personal growth, as well as address the gray areas and challenges that arise when navigating casual sexual relationships. Stay tuned as we continue to uncover the many layers of the hookup culture and the truths that lie within.

Chapter 2
Unraveling the Stigma: Embracing Sexual Freedom

Casual sex has long been associated with cultural stigmas and judgments. It is stashed away in whispered conversations and swept beneath the carpet.

For far too long, individuals have been suffocated by the shame and guilt associated with exploring one's sexuality outside of traditional relationships.

However, it may be time to question these traditions and embrace sexual freedom without judgment. To completely comprehend society's attitudes about casual sex, we must first recognize the significant influence of cultural and religious beliefs on our sense of relationships. Established institutions have taught about morality, fidelity, and the sacredness of monogamy for generations.

These doctrines have permeated our collective psyche, causing us to regard casual sex as abnormal and morally wrong. It is, nonetheless, critical to address these beliefs objectively. Consensual casual sex causes what genuine harm?

We can begin to address long-held assumptions and tackle the prejudices that obscure our judgment by engaging in open and honest talks.

The feminist movement has also had a big impact on how we view casual sex. Women are now liberated to accept their sexual impulses and push for sexual freedom as they have broken free from old gender roles.

This transition has driven many people to question traditional norms and celebrate their autonomy in making decisions about their bodies and relationships.

Accepting sexual freedom allows people to recover their power and reject the concept that their worth is determined by their sexual behavior.

It is a self-affirming gesture as well as a step toward breaking free from obsolete conventions. We must create an environment in which everyone feels comfortable and empowered to pursue their dreams without fear of being judged or shamed. It is critical to separate the act of casual sex from the negative connotations that have been attached to it. It requires consent, respect, and open communication, just like any other intimate encounter. It is critical to establish clear limits and expectations in order to ensure a positive and empowering experience for all persons involved.

 As we challenge societal norms surrounding casual sex, we must also dispel the myth that it inevitably leads to empty, unfulfilling encounters.

While some may choose casual sex as a means of exploring their sexuality or satisfying physical desires, others may find genuine connections and emotional fulfillment in these experiences.

It is critical to recognize that relationships and intimacy take many forms, and the importance we place on them should not be undercut by cultural stereotypes.

Accepting sexual freedom allows society to become more tolerant and accepting. It necessitates letting go of preconceived notions and allowing individuals to live truthfully, without shame or guilt. We can only genuinely appreciate the intricacies of human desire and build a culture of understanding and acceptance if we break the silence and challenge the stigmas associated with casual sex. To do this, we can take the following practical steps: Open Conversations Should Be Made More Common: Encourage frank conversations about sex, relationships, and sexuality.

We may educate and enlighten ourselves by creating safe spaces for discourse, dispelling myths and lowering judgment and stigma. Give Comprehensive Sexual Education: Stress the significance of sex education that extends beyond abstinence-only teachings.

We can empower folks to engage in consensual and responsible sexual experiences by providing extensive and inclusive education. Consent should be prioritized: Emphasize the importance of willing consent as the foundation of any sexual interaction.

Discuss the significance of good communication, knowing boundaries, and valuing personal liberty in order to create healthy and empowering experiences.

Encourage the formation of supportive networks where individuals can locate like-minded persons who accept sexual freedom without condemnation. These groups can offer tools, support, and a sense of belonging, allowing people to explore their inclinations without feeling ashamed. Address Gender-Based Double Standards: Address the gender-based double standards that persist in society when it comes to casual sex.

To build a more accepting and nonjudgmental environment, promote equality and combat the assumption that women who embrace their sexuality are "slut-shamed" while males are celebrated. Work to Promote Consent Culture: Advocate for a larger social movement toward consent culture, highlighting the significance of active, continuous permission in all sexual relationships. We may build healthier and more meaningful friendships by embracing and advocating the values of consent.

Encourage individuals to prioritize their own desires and agency when it comes to their sexual experiences by empowering personal agency. Because each person's path is unique, it is critical to empower people to make decisions that are consistent with their own values and objectives, free of external judgment. Celebrate Diversity: Emphasize the importance of honoring the wide spectrum of human sexuality experiences and preferences. Encourage inclusivity and acceptance for all consensual sexual expressions, while keeping in mind that what works for one person may not work for another.

By taking these actions, we may begin to break down the stigma associated with casual sex and develop a society that values sexual freedom and personal autonomy. We are paving the road for a more understanding, caring, and inclusive society in which people may accept their desires without fear or guilt.

Chapter 3
The Hoe Phase Defined: Understanding the Concept

One word that has acquired prevalence in today's ever-changing dating market is "hoe phase." This notion, which is frequently surrounded by controversy and misinformation, merits closer consideration in order to completely appreciate its meaning and relevance. We hope that by going into the depths of the hoe phase, we can shed light on its nuances and provide a more nuanced perspective for people who are interested in the subject of casual sex and relationships.

The term "hoe phase" is widely used to characterize a time in someone's life, usually during their adolescence, when they indulge in casual sexual experiences but have no desire for meaningful partnerships. It's important to note that the hoe phase isn't only for one gender; it can be enjoyed by people of different genders, sexual orientations, and backgrounds.

The hoe phase has evolved in the modern dating environment as a result of a variety of causes, including evolving societal standards, more sexual liberation, and the expanding influence of hookup culture. It is critical to consider the hoe phase as a personal choice that some people make to explore their sexuality and wants outside of the limits of a traditional committed partnership.

Understanding the relevance of the hoe phase necessitates an appreciation for the complexities of human sexuality.

For some, the home phase serves as a way of self-discovery, allowing them to gain a clear understanding of their preferences, constraints, and desires. It enables individuals to explore their own bodies, try out new sensations, and get a better awareness of their sexual needs.

Furthermore, the hoe phase can be crucial in confronting traditional norms and stigmas around sex and relationships. Individuals regain their individuality and reject the concept that one's self-worth is primarily determined by their romantic involvement or lack thereof by engaging in consensual casual encounters. It is a daring act of self-expression that demonstrates that sexual exploration can coexist with emotional independence and personal growth.

However, it is critical to note that the hoe phase is not a one-size-fits-all experience. Despite its empowering features, it may also be a moment of uncertainty, vulnerability, and self-doubt. Casual sex can occasionally blur the borders between physical pleasure and emotional connection, resulting in possible emotional distress or contradicting expectations. To ensure the home phase stays a pleasant experience, it is critical to manage these issues with open communication, permission, and self-awareness.

As our understanding of connections evolves, it is critical to approach the next phase without bias or previous preconceptions. Instead, we should promote open talks that validate the experiences of people who are exploring their sexuality in various ways. We may demolish old moral assumptions and appreciate the various ways people express their wishes by building empathy and understanding.

Finally, the hoe phase is a topic worth exploring and comprehending, particularly for those interested in the changing dynamics of sex and relationships. We seek to challenge traditional standards, empower individuals on their sexual journeys, and build a more open and accepting society by defining and delving into the intricacies of the hoe phase. So let's go on this adventure together, uncovering the secrets behind the hoe phase and understanding the enormous impact it has on today's dating scene.

As we continue to investigate the hoe phase and its significance in today's dating market, it is critical to consider the various obstacles and objections that come with this idea. While it is critical to validate and empower individuals throughout this stage of their sexual journey, it is also critical to recognize the intricacies and potential traps that may develop.

One of the main worries about the hoe phase is the possibility of emotional effects. Casual sex without the desire for serious partnerships can cause a blurring of the lines between physical pleasure and emotional connection. It is not uncommon for people to experience conflicted expectations, unrequited feelings, or a sense of emptiness following casual meetings. It is critical to emphasize that emotional vulnerability is not restricted to committed relationships. Casual sex can sometimes make people feel exposed and vulnerable. To navigate these emotional complexities, honest communication, self-awareness, and a commitment to practicing consent are required.

Furthermore, the hoe phase raises concerns about the potential health hazards of casual sexual relations. It is critical to prioritize sexual health by engaging in safe sex, using protection, and being tested for sexually transmitted infections (STIs) on a regular basis. Everyone should take responsibility for their sexual health and be aware of the dangers of casual sexual activity.

Individuals in the hoe phase may face additional problems such as societal judgment and stigma. Despite advances in sexual autonomy and equality, there are still stereotypes and double standards around casual sex. Judgmental attitudes against persons who embrace their sexuality outside of traditional relationships can result in emotions of shame, guilt, and social exclusion. It is critical to overcome these stigmas and develop a more welcoming and inclusive culture that values individual sexuality choices and autonomy.

To successfully get beyond the hoe phase, one must also learn to value consent in all sexual relations. Healthy and respectful sexual encounters are built on the foundation of consent. The ability to establish personal boundaries, communicate one's goals, and revoke one's permission is a fundamental human right. It is critical to develop open lines of communication and guarantee the full support and agreement of all parties.

The long-term implications of the hoe phase on one's future relationships are another factor to keep in mind. Casual sex and exploration has the potential to be both freeing and empowering, but it may also alter one's perspective on monogamy, commitment, and intimacy.

It might be difficult for some people to move on from the more carefree home period into a more conventional committed partnership. Navigating this change and establishing healthy, mutually gratifying relationships requires honesty, self-reflection, and open conversation with potential partners.

Overall, the hoe phase is a complex idea that calls for your full attention. It provides people with a safe space to experiment with their sexuality, question accepted standards, and reclaim control over their bodies. However, it is essential to be aware of the emotional sensitivity, health concerns, societal judgment, and impact on future relationships that may occur during this phase. Individuals can prioritize their own physical and mental well-being while navigating the home phase if they come to it with an attitude of open communication, self-awareness, and a commitment to consent. In the end, the home phase is just one expression of personal inquiry in the ever-changing environment of modern dating, and the road to self-discovery and sexual liberation is different for everyone. It's time to take stock of what we've learned about the hoe phase and recognize the variety of ways people experience and express sexuality.

Chapter 4
Unveiling the Myth: Separating Fact from Fiction

There are few issues more misunderstood and sensationalized in the realm of casual sex and relationships as the infamous "hoe phase." There are several misconceptions around this word, which is used to characterize a time in a person's life when they frequently have sexual encounters that do not lead to more committed relationships. In this chapter, we'll try to dispel these fallacies, correct common misunderstandings, and shed light on the hoe phase based on hard data.

The idea that the hoe phase only affects females is a frequent fallacy regarding this era. This false belief holds that only females are capable of casual sex and self-discovery. But the truth is that the hoe phase doesn't care about your gender. This stage is open to people of all gender identities and expressions, including men and women. We can learn less about human diversity and sexual exploration if we believe it is a stage limited to one gender.

Another common misconception about the hoe phase is that those going through it have no pride or no self-esteem. This false belief suggests that engaging in casual sexual activity lowers one's value. However, remember that consenting casual encounters are perfectly acceptable and can even be beneficial to your sexual health. Assuming someone's value due to their sexual orientation is not only discriminatory, but also contributes to a culture of shame and condemnation.

The hoe phase is also misinterpreted as an indication of sexual irresponsibility. This falsehood holds that people who engage in casual sex activities lack emotional maturity and dedication. However, the truth is that people in the home phase might feel and think about relationships in a variety of ways. Some may be testing the waters of their sexual appetites and pushing the limits of their comfort zones, while others may simply be relishing the independence that comes with engaging in casual relationships rather than actively seeking more committed partnerships.

When addressing the hoe phase, it is essential to distinguish between fact and fantasy. We can learn more about how people handle casual sexual encounters and relationships if we do this. Then we can finally get over the stigmas and assumptions that have been attached to this subject for so long.

Later in this chapter, we'll explore further into the nuances of the hoe phase, analyzing the psychological factors, cultural influences, and individual experiences that create this exploratory stage. We hope that this balanced examination of the hoe phase's pros and cons will help readers form a more nuanced opinion about the experience and its value.

As we enter the second half of this chapter, get ready to go on a trip that peels back the layers of reality, tests the presumptions, and illuminates the various experiences inside the home phase. Our goal is to provide our readers with sufficient background information and evidence-based views to help them reach their own conclusions about this hotly contested issue.

The barriers to progress and mutual understanding can only be removed if we first break the silence and expose the reality. In the next section, we'll examine how the hoe phase is shaped by a complex interweaving of individual experience and cultural norms. What lies ahead, though, will change how you view this mysterious period.In this chapter's latter part, we delve deeper into the complicated nature of the hoe phase, tracing its roots back to both individual experience and societal norms. We believe that by going deeper into this topic, we can provide our readers a fuller picture of the hoe phase and its impact on those who go through it.

The hoe period is sometimes wrongly associated with shallowness of character or sexual immaturity. It's important to keep in mind that while some people may have sexual interactions on the side without looking for anything more, others may come to profoundly value their experiences and build meaningful friendships at this time. The home phase can be a time of discovery, self-improvement, and the emergence of meaningful relationships for certain people.

It's worth thinking about how the hoe phase isn't a universally experienced stage. The journeys of all people are different because they are molded by the desires, experiences, and circumstances of the travelers themselves. Recognizing the variety within this stage allows us to move beyond simplistic generalizations about the people who participate in casual sexual activity and the reasons they do so.

The hoe phase is significantly shaped by societal factors as well. How people experience and negotiate this period can be profoundly affected by cultural norms, media portrayals, and societal expectations related to sexuality.

People may feel safer and more comfortable exploring their sexuality in societies that promote sex positivity and encourage honest dialogue about consent, boundaries, and sexual health.

However, in cultures where sex is taboo, where frank discussion of wants is frowned upon, or where gender inequality prevails, people may feel pushed to hide their experiences during the home period or adapt to social norms.

These factors can amplify negative attitudes toward casual sexual encounters and lead to the spread of harmful stigmas.

Personal memories and experiences are also important to explore when trying to make sense of the home phase. Culture, upbringing, connections, and personal ideals all play a part in shaping an individual's path. Listening to these accounts is a great way to learn about the experiences of people from all walks of life who have gone through the "hoe" era.

Our hope is that by giving these people a louder voice, we can help dismantle harmful stereotypes, increase compassion, and create a culture that respects people's right to make their own decisions about their sexuality. The importance of giving these narratives a voice and giving them the attention and respect they deserve cannot be overstated.

As this chapter comes to a close, we want readers to consider their own preconceived notions regarding the hoe phase. In order to break the silence and expose the truths behind this mysterious period, we must all work together to eliminate the biases and misunderstandings that stand in the way of our development and comprehension.

We think that by bringing light to the many facets of the hoe phase, we will encourage more candid discussions about sex without commitment. This is the only way to build a culture that accepts and supports everyone, no matter their sexual orientation or gender identity.

Understanding the significance of dialogue, agreement, and introspection during the home stage is the subject of the next chapter. Come discuss ways to promote mental health, individual development, and positive sexual encounters via open communication and the establishment of healthy boundaries.

As we move on, keep in mind that the hoe phase is only one thread in the intricate tapestry that is the sexual development of humans. We need to end the taboo, reveal the facts, and encourage a more open dialogue regarding casual sexual encounters and partnerships. In the following chapter, we'll discuss the home phase in greater detail, including the nuances of communication, consent, and self-discovery.

Chapter 5
Emotional Well-being: Navigating Casual Relationships

Casual dating is all the rage in today's modern dating scene. More and more people are choosing casual hookups over serious relationships, thanks in part to the proliferation of dating apps and a general shift in cultural mores. Casual relationships have the potential to be liberating and exhilarating, but they also have their own emotional challenges. In this chapter, we will examine the psychological facets of casual relationships, including how to stay healthy and deal with stress.

Maintaining mental and emotional health is essential for negotiating casual partnerships. Keep in mind that even in casual relationships, feelings can run high. It's crucial to be in touch with yourself and conscious of your emotions when pursuing casual relationships. Spend some time contemplating what you hope to gain from these interactions so that you may better prepare yourself for the emotional terrain.

Having healthy emotional boundaries in casual relationships is important. Talk to your partner freely and honestly about what you want from the relationship and what you can offer. It is essential to determine what each party will and will not accept. Exclusiveness, how often you talk, and your emotional availability are all good things to discuss. Doing so lessens the chance of miscommunication and future heartache.

In order to keep one's emotional stability in casual relationships, self-care is essential. Be kind to yourself and put your own needs first.

Spend some time doing things that make you happy, whether it's interacting with loved ones, following a hobby, or simply reflecting on your life. This is important for more than just avoiding emotional exhaustion; it also aids in the development of an independent sense of value.

It can be difficult to navigate the emotional terrain of casual relationships, especially if feelings for your partner begin to emerge. Emotions are normal and healthy; there's no need to bury them. Feel what you're feeling and accept it, but try to limit the impact it has on your decisions. Realize that just because you're starting to feel strongly for someone in a casual relationship doesn't indicate they feel the same way.

Positive emotional health in casual relationships also depends on open lines of communication. Communicate your feelings to your partner openly and honestly. Don't be afraid to speak up about your worries and thoughts. It's crucial for all parties to be on the same page, thus open communication is essential. Express your sentiments to your spouse if you're feeling overwhelmed or that your feelings are at odds with the informal nature of your connection. When people are truthful with one another, they gain a better grasp on the other's feelings.

The ability to adapt to changing circumstances is crucial in casual partnerships. There may be times when you feel jealous, insecure, or afraid of rejection. These feelings should not be ignored but rather confronted head-on. If you need help working through your emotions, talk to friends or a therapist. Keep in mind that feeling a wide range of emotions is completely normal, and that it is essential for your mental health to recognize and appropriately process all of them.

It is important to keep in mind the uniqueness of each person's experience as we delve into the emotional facets of casual relationships. What helps one individual may not help another. It's crucial to recognize the importance of your own mental health and make it a top priority. Maintaining a healthy emotional balance in the midst of the ups and downs of casual relationships is possible via the use of healthy boundary-setting, self-care, and open communication.

In the next portion of this chapter, we will go deeper into the intangibles of casual relationships and offer more advice on how to stay happy and cope with difficulties.

Expectation management is crucial for emotional health in casual partnerships. It's crucial to recognize that casual relationships aren't the same as committed partnerships in terms of commitment and exclusivity. It's important for both parties to come into the relationship with clear goals and expectations. This makes it less likely that there will be any misunderstandings or letdowns later on.

Self-awareness and introspection are additional methods for maintaining mental health. Maintain a frequent self-checking routine. Consider how you feel and whether or not this casual relationship serves your needs and principles. Keeping your mental health in mind at all times is of paramount importance. It's important to evaluate the casual relationship and consider ending it if it's giving you emotional suffering or disrupting your emotional stability.

Understanding and being okay with the possibility of developing feelings is another crucial part of negotiating casual relationships. Because of our complexity as human beings, it is only normal for us to feel something in even casual relationships. It's important to keep lines of communication open with your partner whenever feelings like this surface. Communicating your true feelings to someone doesn't always indicate you're moving toward a more committed partnership. Both people can better navigate the emotional landscape if they are honest about their feelings and experiences.

For psychological health, it's also important to make time for people you care about outside of your casual relationships. If you need help, lean on reliable friends or get it from a professional. When figuring out how to handle the nuances of a casual relationship, it helps to have someone to talk to about it. Having someone else to talk to about difficult feelings like envy or rejection can be really helpful.

Remember that checking in on the causal relationship's status on a regular basis may be necessary to ensure your emotional well-being. It's important to check in on how the arrangement is serving your emotional needs on a regular basis because feelings and situations might shift over time. Constantly checking in with one another to assess progress ensures that both parties are on the same page at all times.

In conclusion, maintaining your mental health is essential for negotiating the tricky terrain of platonic friendships. Individuals can keep their emotional equilibrium by setting realistic goals, learning to accept and embrace change, being honest with themselves and others, and reaching out for help when they need it. It's important to keep in mind that everyone's journey is different and that one person's success formula may not apply to another. Put your emotional health first, and use honesty, clarity, and self-compassion as you negotiate casual relationships.

Chapter 6
Communication: Setting Boundaries and Expectations

No matter the nature of the relationship, great outcomes can only be achieved via open and honest communication. Casual relationships, like those that occur during the dreaded "hoe phase," increase the importance of open dialogue. Misunderstandings, breached boundaries, and unmet expectations are all possible outcomes when people fail to express themselves clearly. Managing expectations and establishing limits through open dialogue is the emphasis of this chapter on communication in casual relationships.

Casual relationships are less about making a long-term commitment and more about having fun and finding out who you really are. Relationships that focus primarily on physical intimacy can be casual hookups, friends with benefits, or everything in between. However, despite the lack of commitment, it is still crucial for these partnerships to have open and honest communication.

In casual relationships, communication is especially important when it comes to setting limits. Having clear boundaries allows couples to safely explore their sexual impulses while still honoring one another's individuality and space needs. Without clear limits in place, one partner may inadvertently cross the line into unacceptable territory, damaging the trust between them.

Boundaries can only be set via open and honest communication. Everyone should feel safe enough to share their needs, wants, and boundaries without worrying about being misunderstood or rejected. It's important to make sure that there's a place for honest communication between the two of you. The key to accomplishing this is laying the groundwork for trust and mutual respect, with an emphasis on the importance of honest dialogue to the success of all parties involved.

Setting limits and controlling expectations are both crucial in casual relationships. People enter into these types of partnerships with a variety of goals in mind. It's possible that some people are looking for a serious long-term relationship, while others are hoping for something more casual and merely physical. Disappointment, resentment, and even the breakup of a relationship are all possible outcomes of having unrealistic expectations. It's important for partners in a casual relationship to talk early on about what they hope to get out of it.

This ensures that all parties are on the same page and that any potential misconceptions are eliminated. It's not easy to broach the topic of expectations, but doing so early on can prevent a lot of hurt feelings down the road.

Constant dialogue and evaluation are also necessary for effective expectation management. Emotions, goals, and life situations might shift over time. Therefore, it is important to make sure that your expectations are in line with the present status of your relationship by having regular check-in conversations. Adjustments may be made and unfulfilled demands can be avoided with the help of this constant two-way communication.

In conclusion, strong relationships, including casual ones, are built on a foundation of open and honest communication. Communication in casual relationships is essential for setting limits and managing expectations. When both partners are on the same page about the nature and future of the relationship, it is much easier to establish clear limits that make exploration seem secure.

As we go more into the issue of communication in casual relationships, we will examine many methods that can be used to successfully navigate these types of talks. In this chapter's second part, you'll learn useful advice for improving your communication skills and how to overcome some of the most typical obstacles you're likely to encounter.

Let's focus on the value of open dialogue in laying a solid groundwork for casual relationships for the time being. The second half of this chapter will focus on more specific advice for communicating well in informal interactions, as well as addressing typical difficulties that may develop.

In informal connections, listening is one of the most crucial communication skills. Both partners need to be willing to listen attentively to one another in order to fully comprehend and cater to one another's requirements. This is giving your undivided attention to the person speaking without interrupting them or diverting your attention elsewhere. Paying attention to the speaker's nonverbal clues, such as their body language and tone of voice, is an important part of active listening. To avoid confusion and miscommunication, it's important for both parties to develop the skill of active listening.

Using "I" statements is another important part of good communication. Using "I" words might help you avoid seeming accusatory or judgemental while communicating your wants, needs, and limits. It's possible for people to communicate their wants and requirements without resorting to confrontation by using phrases like "I feel uncomfortable when..." or "I would like it if..." Taking this tack increases the likelihood of honest communication and decreases the likelihood of defensive responses.

In addition, it's crucial for casual relationships to keep the lines of communication open. To better assess and communicate any shifts in wants, needs, or limits, it's helpful to check in on a regular basis. All participants in these discussions should feel safe enough to speak their minds without fear of repercussion. Partners can better meet one another's needs and make the connection work by keeping lines of communication open.

Problems can occur in casual relationships despite our best intentions. The inability to open up and trust others is a common obstacle. For fear of being judged or rejected, many people hide their genuine emotions and desires. It's important to foster an atmosphere where neither partner feels threatened by the other's opinions or criticisms, so that honest communication may take place. Intimacy and trust can flourish when partners are encouraged to be vulnerable with one another.

The development of romantic sentiments for the other person is another potential complication. Many people enter into casual relationships with the expectation that they will be short-lived and low-commitment. Nonetheless, emotions may emerge out of nowhere at times. When this occurs, being upfront and honest about how you feel is crucial. Each person in the relationship should think about how they feel and whether or not they are ready to move toward a more committed arrangement.

In conclusion, it is essential for both partners in a casual relationship to be able to express their needs, wants, and limits to one another. Essential elements of good communication include active listening, the use of "I" statements, continuous communication, and the creation of a safe environment for vulnerability. Even if difficulties develop, communicating openly and honestly can aid a partnership in resolving them. The health of casual relationships depends on open dialogue in which boundaries are acknowledged and expectations are well managed.

We will continue our discussion of sustaining mental health in casual relationships in the future chapter. We'll talk about the value of knowing oneself, taking care of oneself, and developing positive coping strategies. Stay tuned as we reveal the keys to thriving in the "hoe phase" and finding happiness in fleeting relationships.

Chapter 7
Consent and Respect: Ensuring Safe Encounters

Consent and respect should never be compromised in the complex terrain of chance encounters, when desires entwine and passions flame. This seemingly basic idea is often misinterpreted or disregarded, with potentially disastrous results and a consequent erosion of confidence. This chapter explores the value of consent and courtesy in everyday interactions, with the goal of fostering an environment where people feel safe talking to one another and may share their experiences openly.

The core of consent is a freely offered agreement between all parties. It's a never-ending procedure that requires positivity, clarity, and knowledge. Consent is the cornerstone of any good relationship, because without it, not only are the people involved autonomy and well-being disregarded, but so is the trust that sustains it. Because of the potential for misunderstanding and injury in the context of casual encounters, it is especially important to speak clearly and gain each other's consent.

Consensual interactions can only flourish when based on mutual respect. It's more than just "giving others the same consideration you'd like to be given." To treat others with respect in informal situations, one must take into account their specific needs, preferences, and limits. It requires paying close attention, feeling sympathetic towards the other person, and wanting their happiness over your own. We can ensure that everyone feels safe and heard, and that their needs and boundaries will not be violated if we promote a culture of respect.

Having honest and open conversations can go a long way toward building trust and understanding. Before beginning a romantic relationship, it's important for both partners to be completely open and honest about their wants, needs, and limits. This demands bravery and openness on all parts, but it is essential to laying the groundwork for trust and mutual understanding. Consent is never taken for granted, no matter how comfortable you are with someone or how long you've known them. Verbalizing consent should become second nature to establish a shared understanding and limit the chance of misunderstandings or breached boundaries, especially given the one-of-a-kind character of each interaction.

Furthermore, consent is not a static state but rather an ongoing procedure that takes place all during the interaction. It's important to check in with one another to make sure everyone is still enjoying themselves and feeling welcome in the group. The non-verbal indications our partners provide us about their emotional condition and degree of comfort are just as important as the words we exchange. When everyone's space and rights are respected, it's easier to feel safe opening out to one another.

We may give ourselves and others the confidence to have genuine, consensual encounters if we foster an environment of safety and mutual understanding. Every person's wishes and boundaries, regardless of their gender, sexual orientation, or society expectations, should be respected. This includes challenging societal norms and prejudices surrounding casual sex and relationships.

Let's shatter the quiet and make it so that respectful, open dialogue about consent is the rule rather than the exception. Respect is something that must be gained and not given.

Respect, however, should be a precondition at the commencement of any informal meeting. Without respect, it is possible to breach others' boundaries, act without their consent, and cause them pain. This section of the chapter will go more deeply into the significance of respect in facilitating pleasant and secure interactions.

All polite and consensual interactions must begin with self-respect. Before interacting with people, it is essential to have a firm grasp on one's own limits, preferences, and wants. Being aware of and secure in one's own wants and requirements facilitates effective communication and negotiation with prospective partners. Prioritizing our own happiness isn't egocentric; rather, it's a prerequisite for thriving in both short- and long-term connections.

Recognizing and honoring the space and independence of others is crucial as well. Consent is a mutual agreement, not a bargaining position. It involves agreeing with the other person's choice to join or not in an activity and not trying to force them to change their minds. Consent is also understood to be revocable at any time and should be respected without inquiry. By valuing each other's independence, we can create a welcoming community where people feel confident sharing their needs, wants, and boundaries without being judged or pressured.

Recognizing the potential for unequal power dynamics is crucial to fostering healthy interactions. Age, income, social prestige, and emotional sensitivity are all potential causes of power imbalances. These differences should never be utilized to trick others into lowering their guard or crossing your own lines. When interacting with strangers, it's important to keep power dynamics in mind and treat everyone as an equal participant in the decision-making process.

Furthermore, courteous discourse goes beyond the confines of a single interaction. All aspects of our behavior leading up to, during, and following close interactions with another person are included. When we communicate mindfully, we tell each other the truth about what we want, where we draw the line, and how we feel after the conversation has ended. It's not just a kind thing to do; it also helps people feel comfortable talking to one another openly and honestly, laying the groundwork for future interactions based on mutual respect and understanding.

It is necessary to confront societal norms and assumptions around casual sex and relationships on the path to fostering a culture of safety and mutual understanding. Contempt and shame can further fuel destructive dynamics and shut down honest dialogue about mutual respect and consent. By recognizing the value in differences, challenging preconceived notions, and honoring each person's right to set their own limits, we can foster an environment where everyone may feel safe to be themselves.

In conclusion, mutual respect and understanding are the bedrock of positive and fruitful chance meetings. We can foster an environment where everyone's voice is heard, personal space is respected, and accepted differences are celebrated. Keep in mind that gaining someone's consent is an ongoing procedure that necessitates treating them with respect. The silence must be broken, a culture of safety and respect must be fostered, and every casual interaction must be safe, healthy, and respectful.

Chapter 8
Navigating Insecurities: Self-Reflection and Empowerment

It's normal for doubts to crop up in casual relationships. When we're feeling vulnerable and uncertain, it's natural to question our value and worth. It's important to keep in mind, though, that working through your fears is ultimately a path to greater self-awareness and strength. Insecurities are normal in casual relationships, and this chapter will address them and offer solutions for dealing with them via self-improvement, empowerment, and introspection.

The feeling of being inadequate is a frequent issue that can arise in casual relationships. Because of how casually they are formed, questions about commitment can slip into these relationships. Concerns like, "Am I attractive enough?" or "Will they lose interest in me?" may be constantly running through our heads.

The first step in overcoming this uneasiness is to appreciate who we are and the value we provide to the world. Realize that you don't need anything else to be happy. Put your energy into building a positive sense of self and doing things that bring you joy. Learn to validate yourself and recognize your own skills and traits rather than depending exclusively on external validation.

Fear of being categorized or judged is another common source of uneasiness. There is a certain stigma attached to the term "hoe phase" that causes people to second-guess themselves and worry about what others may think. Keep in mind that other people's opinions don't have to shape who you are.

Take charge of your life by accepting and being at peace with the decisions you've made. Keep in mind that you should not let the judgments of others stop you from following your heart. Surround yourself with positive people who will help you grow and learn about yourself as you explore the world.

It's also possible for concerns to originate from a reluctance to become emotionally invested in a casual relationship. When we let our guard down emotionally, we leave ourselves up to hurt and disappointment. It's crucial to acknowledge these worries and deal with them through introspection and openness.

Spend some time thinking about yourself so you can identify your emotional requirements and set appropriate limits. Make sure you and your spouse are on the same page by having frank conversations about what you want from the relationship. Keep in mind that if we face our own and others' vulnerabilities with confidence and wisdom, we can gain strength from them.

Casual relationships might be fraught with insecurities, but they're not insurmountable. Accepting oneself and actively seeking out connections that support one's values and goals are the hallmarks of personal empowerment. We can overcome fears and set off on a rewarding road of casual relationships if we take the time to ponder, develop, and increase our sense of value.

To overcome this fear, keep in mind that being rejected is not indicative of who you really are. Every person makes decisions based on a unique set of priorities and experiences. Focus on developing yourself instead than worrying about being turned down. Use this time to better yourself by learning more about who you are, what you're interested in, and how to build your own self-assurance. You can strengthen your ability to cope with rejection by prioritizing your own pleasure and growth.

Having frank and open discussions about your hopes and feelings with your partner is also essential. You can make the environment safer and more pleasant for both of you if you take the time to learn about each other's goals and expectations. The discomfort associated with rejection and uncertainty may be lessened via such candid discussion. No matter how casual your relationship is, remember that open communication is vital to its success.

The insecurity caused by the dread of being compared to others is also relevant. It is easy to doubt ourselves and compare our "body count" or experiences to others in a society that places so much emphasis on numbers and statistics when it comes to personal encounters. Feelings of shame and inadequacy might result from the worry of failing to live up to society standards.

Realize that your value is not based on statistics or approval from others. The experiences of others should not be compared to or evaluated against one's own. Regardless of what other people may think or say, you should embrace and appreciate your own journey. Remember that true empowerment comes from inside, not from external validation, and surround yourself with people who appreciate and uplift your decisions.

Lack of resolution in casual relationships can sometimes cause insecurities. Due to the lack of clarity and structure in these relationships, each party involved may have been left wondering if they even mattered to the other. Keep in mind that putting an end to something isn't always necessary for moving on with your life.

If the person you're seeking closure from is unwilling or unable to give it, your search will likely result in more frustration and pain. Instead, you should work on coming to terms with your own feelings. Think about how you've changed and how much you've contributed to the relationship. Realize that it's acceptable to let go and that sometimes closure comes from realizing that not all relationships are intended to last.

Finally, learning to deal with fears in casual relationships is an exercise in introspection and agency. Individuals can start down a path toward growth and fulfillment after they become aware of and work over their common fears, such as the fear of not being enough, judgment anxiety, attachment anxiety, rejection anxiety, comparison anxiety, and lack of closure. You can gain self-assurance and control over your life by realizing your value, being honest with yourself and others, building relationships with positive people, and solving any unresolved issues you may have. In this way, you can confidently and clearly negotiate the difficulties of casual relationships.

Chapter 9
Sexual Health: Prioritizing Well-being and Protection

It is essential to put one's sexual health first when participating in casual sex and relationships, as it is an integral part of one's overall well-being. It is essential to discuss the significance of safe practices, STI prevention, and routine testing in order to sustain a healthy and joyful sexual life.

Safe sex practices are crucial to maintaining sexual health. Casual sexual activity raises the risk of contracting a sexually transmitted infection (STI) if standard safety measures are not followed. In order to lessen the likelihood of transmission, barrier techniques like condoms and dental dams must be used. These safety measures not only help avoid unwanted pregnancies, but they also guard against sexually transmitted infections. Regular and proper condom use ensures that sexual experiences are both pleasurable and risk-free.

Talking openly and honestly with your partner(s) about your sexual health is also essential. Before engaging in sexual activity, it's important to talk about sexual history, STI testing, and any previous encounters. Because of this openness, people are able to make educated choices regarding their sexual health. Although having these discussions may make some people feel uneasy, it is essential to ensure everyone's wellbeing.

All sexually active people should make regular STI testing a part of their practice. It is feasible to avoid getting a sexually transmitted infection (STI) by constantly engaging in safe sex practices. It's possible for some illnesses to be asymptomatic, or show no outward symptoms at all. Early diagnosis and treatment greatly reduces the potential for problems and spread, so it's important to get checked often. The ability to make educated judgments about one's sexual health and the confidence to engage in casual sexual encounters are both enhanced by knowing one's STI status.

In addition to following best practices and getting checked often, it's also important to take care of your general health. Taking care of one's body, heart, and head are all part of this. Self-care practices including regular exercise, stress management, and enough sleep have been linked to improved sexual encounters. Taking care of oneself in a holistic manner improves sexual health, leading to more satisfying and pleasurable interactions between partners.

It's important to note that sex health encompasses more than just the body; it also includes the mind and spirit. Communication and boundary-setting in casual sexual encounters are paramount. When people make an effort to learn about one another's wants, needs, and expectations, everyone benefits. Sexual and mental fulfillment are intertwined with our emotional health.

The more we learn, the more we realize that sexual health is complex and calls for wide-ranging intervention. The purpose of this chapter is to educate readers about the significance of engaging in healthy, safe, and respectful sexual practices and relationships. By giving these things top priority, people can confidently and mindfully face the challenges of their sexual lives.

Halfway through the chapter...)It is important to go deeper into the concept of consent as we continue our investigation of sexual health in the context of casual sex and partnerships. All participants involved in a sexual interaction should give their informed consent voluntarily and with enthusiasm. No one's permission should ever be taken for granted, and anyone can revoke it at any time. Maintaining a safe and affirming sexual environment requires mutual respect for personal space and open lines of communication.

Consent is not a binary "yes" or "no" to a series of discrete actions; rather, it is an open and evolving set of relationships. It calls on both parties to get involved and maintain an open line of communication. Knowing that consent can be withdrawn at any time, even in the midst of a sexual interaction, is crucial. A single act of consent does not constitute assent to any and all future acts.

Being aware of one's own and one's partner(s)' emotional needs and experiences is essential in establishing a safe and respectful setting for sexual exploration. For a romantic relationship to thrive, emotional closeness and trust must first be established. The quality of sexual encounters can be improved by prioritizing emotional health and trust building.

For psychological health and making a sexually inviting environment, nothing beats open dialogue. It is essential to have frank conversations about wants, limits, and expectations with a relationship or partners. Because it fosters comprehension and a closer bond between partners, it makes for a more joyful and rewarding sexual experience.

Self-reflection and self-awareness are important factors in fostering healthy casual sexual relationships alongside open communication and mutual consent. It's crucial to take stock of our sexual lives on a frequent basis and see if they're in line with our wants and requirements. Making educated decisions about one's sexual health and making any required adjustments to one's limits or habits can be facilitated by regular reflection.

Furthermore, we must acknowledge the influence of cultural norms and expectations on our definition of "casual sex" and its link to romantic partnerships. Casual sexual encounters often face judgment and shame in today's society. By questioning these assumptions, people can feel more comfortable expressing their sexuality and enjoying the consequences of their own decisions.

Keep in mind that your experiences and preferences in casual sex and relationships are distinct from everyone else's. Not everyone will benefit from the same approach. Casual sex should be approached with an open mind and a nonjudgmental attitude, and each person's sexual preferences should be respected and validated. The ultimate objective is to foster an environment where casual sexual encounters are characterized by mutual respect, equality, and self-determination.

In conclusion, there are many facets of sexual health that need our attention and care in the context of casual sex and relationships. Each of these factors, from emphasizing mental health and encouraging open communication to engaging in safe sexual practices and being tested often, adds to a satisfying sexual experience. People can approach casual sex and relationships with poise, respect, and awareness if they prioritize consent, open communication, and introspection. Through prioritizing and gaining clarity on these issues, we can disclose the reality behind the alleged "hoe phase."

Chapter 10
When Things Get Complicated: Managing Jealousy and Emotions

Complex emotions like jealousy and envy can be difficult to navigate in the world of casual partnerships, where emotions and connections are generally held at arm's length. Humans have a hardwired propensity for these feelings, and dismissing them in the context of casual relationships would be emotionally insensitive. It's vital to one's emotional well-being to gain insight into and practice effective management of jealousy and envy within these connections. The question then becomes, how do we deal with these feelings as they surface?

Recognizing and recognizing the reality of envy and jealousy is the first step. These feelings are merely expressions of our hopes, anxieties, and uncertainties, and they are not intrinsically bad. The first step toward effectively addressing jealousy and envy is realizing that these are natural human emotions.

The next step is to be completely honest and upfront with your partner or partners. Expressing your own sentiments of envy or jealousy might help you better understand and empathize with others. It's important to let your feelings be known without pointing fingers or making your partner feel bad. Keep in mind that you shouldn't focus on who's at fault, but rather on how you can both move past your feelings.

Understanding the causes of jealousy and envy is one strategy for dealing with these emotions. Think about what's triggering these emotions. Do you worry about drifting apart from your significant other? Do you feel like you have to prove yourself to the other people in a casual relationship?

Insight into your own emotional triggers can be gained by tracing the origins of negative emotions like jealousy and envy back to their origins.

After pinpointing the origin of your negative feelings, it's time to deal with any lingering self-doubt or insecurity. Think about how valuable you are and why you've decided to have a casual relationship. Managing feelings of jealousy and envy requires developing and maintaining a healthy sense of self-worth.

Taking care of yourself is another effective tactic for preventing emotional imbalance. Do things that make you happy, boost your confidence, and improve your health. Taking care of yourself in any way you like (via hobbies, socializing, or introspection) can help you feel better emotionally and mentally.

Keep in mind that even the most casual relationships require clear limits, mutual respect, and trust. Navigating the intricacies of emotions within these connections requires setting and keeping these boundaries. Safe and supportive environments benefit from partners who are open with one another about their needs, wants, and boundaries.

In this chapter's second half, we'll learn more about the complexity of dealing with feelings of jealousy and envy in informal relationships and examine additional ways for doing so. We'll talk about how to deal with feelings of betrayal and how to strengthen your emotional fortitude. As we go deeper into these issues, you'll have access to resources that can help you stay emotionally stable despite the challenges posed by casual relationships.

That being said, let's get started on the path toward mastering the emotions of jealousy and envy so that we can enjoy happier, more rewarding relationships on the side.Let's go deeper into the methods and tools that can help us navigate through jealousy and envy as we continue our investigation into the difficulties of handling these emotions within casual relationships.

If you're dealing with thoughts of envy or jealousy, it can help to keep in mind that both partners in a casual relationship have equal rights to their own independence. A more positive frame of mind begins with this realization. Your spouse or partners have the freedom to pursue interests and friendships outside of your relationship, and you should respect that. When you internalize this knowledge, you can lessen the burden of stress and anxiety.

In addition, it's important to work on building trust in your informal connections. The cornerstone of any positive relationship, whether platonic or otherwise, is trust. For someone to earn another person's trust, they must be dependable and honest, as well as communicative and respectful. You can more easily overcome feelings of

jealousy and envy if you cultivate trust between you and
your partner.

Developing a sense of empathy and compassion can also
help you deal with feelings of envy. Through empathy, we
are able to place ourselves in the other person's position
and grasp their hopes, concerns, and uncertainties. It helps
us put aside our biases and consider things from their point
of view. Compersion, on the other hand, means taking
pleasure in our loved ones' success even if it doesn't
immediately benefit us. By honing these traits, we can
reframe feelings of envy as invitations to deeper
relationships and more shared happiness.

It can be good to learn strategies that strengthen emotional
resilience in order to deal with events that bring on
feelings of jealousy or envy. When feelings are turbulent,
it can help to practice self-soothing techniques like deep
breathing, meditation, or writing. Changing your outlook
and developing a more positive frame of mind can also be
aided by practicing positive self-talk and re-framing
negative beliefs.

Avoiding comparison traps and seeking external approval
are also important. It's not uncommon for people in casual
relationships to date many people at once. Recognize your
own value and the contributions you provide to the
relationship rather than looking for approval from others.
Keep in mind that your value lies not in the adulation of
others but in your own estimation of yourself.

Finally, keep in mind that your mental health is a process,
not an endpoint. It calls for constant introspection and

development. The process of overcoming feelings of envy and jealousy in casual relationships is complex, so be kind to yourself while you work through it. Recognize your successes and take failures as stepping stones to growth and self-awareness.

In conclusion, it might be difficult to manage jealousy and envy in casual relationships, but it is possible to do so via awareness, dialogue, and self-care. In order to successfully navigate the complexities of casual relationships and create healthier and more fulfilling experiences for yourself and your partners, it is important to recognize and accept these emotions; engage in open communication; address underlying insecurities; and cultivate trust, empathy, and resilience.

As we reach the end of this chapter, keep in mind that learning about and controlling these feelings is an ongoing endeavor. We hope that you find the information and advice in this chapter helpful as you work toward emotional health in your casual relationships.

Chapter 11
Friendships with Benefits: Balancing Connection and Intimacy

Traditional ideas of romance and friendship have been challenged by the rise in popularity of casual sex and partnerships. The idea of "friendship with benefits" has become widely accepted in this field. Having sex with a buddy while still being on good terms emotionally is possible. However, the nuances and complexities of such connections are frequently misconstrued.

To successfully navigate a friendship with benefits, both sides need to give the situation serious thought, set clear boundaries, and communicate openly and honestly with one another. It's important to remember that this kind of arrangement can be liberating for certain people by removing the constraints of conventional love obligations and allowing them to experiment with their sexuality. But it also has its own special difficulties and dangers.

It's crucial that people in platonic relationships keep in touch with one another. Talk things out. To make sure that both sides are on the same page, it's important to have open and frank discussions about wants, expectations, and emotional availability. Having clear limits in place from the start will help keep things from getting too difficult between you and your friend.

The effect on your existing relationships is an essential consideration. It's important to evaluate whether or not your activities in a friends-with-benefits relationship are consistent with your values and goals. To avoid damaging other relationships, it's crucial to ask yourself if you're ready for and capable of this level of closeness.

The idea of permission is also crucial to the success of a platonic relationship. All parties involved should be excited about giving their consent on a continuous basis. Never assume that consent is permanent or granted indefinitely, and always respect each other's personal space.

Intimacy within a friend-with-benefits relationship should not be discounted. It may seem counterintuitive, yet even casual interactions can develop into close bonds of affection. Exposing one's emotions and connecting with another person might enrich the experience for both people. It's important to connect emotionally with your friend, yet keep some distance so as not to complicate the friendship.

Accepting the ambiguity and nuance of BFF relationships can be a catalyst for self-discovery and development. It's a chance to go against the grain of conventional wisdom and find out what serves you best. But you should go into this new phase of your life with a healthy dose of self-awareness, emotional maturity, and regard for the happiness of both you and your partner.

The second half of this chapter will go deeper into the difficulties and potential outcomes of BFF relationships. We'll talk about the hazards, the ties that bind, and the techniques for keeping things in perspective. In the upcoming section, we'll delve even further into the

nuances of these connections and provide some insight
into how to successfully navigate the terrain of BFF
relationships.

Beyond the initial problems of communication, limits, and
emotional availability, the difficulties and potential
repercussions of friendships with advantages extend
further. As we progress further into this space, it will be
important to manage the tradeoffs between closeness and
isolation.

The risk that one person will feel more strongly than the
other is significant. Each party may have a firm grasp on
their role in the arrangement, but feelings are never
completely predictable. It's important to check in on how
you're feeling on a frequent basis and have frank
conversations about any changes. If these feelings are
ignored or repressed, they can fester into bitterness, hurt,
and eventually the end of the connection.

The potential effect on one's sense of self-worth is another
danger. It takes courage and assurance to enter into a
friends-with-benefits relationship. Being truthful with
oneself about one's own goals and aspirations is essential.
If one person's feeling of self-worth or pride is being
damaged by the arrangement, it may be time to reconsider
whether or not it is still in everyone's best interests to
maintain it.

The boundaries between platonic and amorous
connections are further muddied by BFFs. While these
feelings are often welcome, they can also lead to some
serious head scratching. Successfully negotiating this

ambiguous space requires honest dialogue and a commitment to self-reflection. This requires both parties to be forthright about their expectations from the partnership and to check in on a frequent basis to make sure their goals are still aligned.

Friendships with advantages require constant two-way communication, not just about the more tangible components of the relationship, but also about the mental and emotional well of both people involved. It's important to check in on a regular basis so that any problems or shifts in wants and needs can be quickly identified. Important choices must be made in an atmosphere where all parties feel safe voicing their opinions and concerns.

Respect and concern for one another are just as crucial as open dialogue. One way to do this is by offering emotional support when required and avoiding actions that could provoke sentiments of jealousy or resentment. Friendship is built on a foundation of mutual respect, which goes far beyond the physical.

Finally, self-awareness, emotional maturity, and mutual respect are essential for thriving in mutual-benefit friendships. It's important to keep your focus on the hazards, your heart in check, and your equilibrium. Maintaining a solid and lasting connection requires open lines of communication, being trustworthy, and checking in regularly. It's an adventure and a chance to develop as a person, but it also takes a dedication to others' happiness.

As we wrap up this chapter, we hope you've learned some important lessons about the subtleties of platonic

friendships with advantages. We have discussed the value
of intimate relationships and the difficulties that can arise
from them. Keep in mind that your experience in this
world will be different from anybody else's, and that it is
ultimately up to you to figure out what works best for you.

Chapter 12
Exiting the Hoe Phase: Transitioning to Different Relationship Styles

Everyone passes through different stages in their relationships. Despite its negative reputation, the home phase can be a time of growth and discovery. It's a moment when people put themselves first and feel free to be sexually expressive and have casual encounters. It's possible that as soon as we start using the hoe, we'll be ready to move on to something else.

Anyone who is ready to move on from the "hoe" phase of relationships and try something new will find helpful information and advice in this section. Introspection, self-awareness, and a willingness to let go of old patterns are necessary for the rewarding journey of shifting from a casual and noncommittal perspective to a more serious and long-lasting approach.

Knowing what you want out of life is the first step out of the home phase. Think about your ideal romantic partner. Do you want someone to share your life with, or do you just want to be with someone? If you know what you want out of a romantic partnership, you can better evaluate your possibilities. It's crucial to be truthful with yourself and recognize any limitations or preconceived notions you may have.

Relationships go through cycles, and each person experiences them differently. The hoe phase is often misunderstood, yet it is actually a period of significant development and self-discovery. It's a time when everyone can be themselves, both in terms of sexual expression and in terms of casual meetings. As soon as we begin using the hoe, we may find that we are eager to go on to other tasks.

This section contains useful information and guidance for anyone who is ready to move on from the "hoe" phase of relationships and try something new. The gratifying path of moving from a casual and noncommittal stance to a more serious and long-lasting attitude requires introspection, self-awareness, and a willingness to let go of previous behaviors.

Identifying your life goals is the first step in moving past the "hoe" stage. Imagine the perfect romantic relationship for you. Do you seek a lifelong companion, or are you content with a casual companion? Having a clear idea of your ideal romantic partner will help you assess your options. It's important to be honest with yourself and acknowledge your own biases and limits.

As we near the end of this chapter's first half, keep in mind that we still have a ways to go. It takes time, introspection, and patience to move on from the home phase and into alternative relationship forms. In the next section, we'll discuss the shift in further detail and offer some tips for making the most of this new and exciting chapter in your relationship. In the next part, we'll talk about how to handle this change in a way that benefits you.

It's not simple to move on from the home phase and into a new kind of connection. It calls for commitment, introspection, and the ability to let go of familiar routines.

In the remaining sections of this chapter, we'll go into further detail about the actions required for this change and offer concrete suggestions for achieving success in this new and exciting era of your relationship.

Learning to respect emotional intimacy and connection is a crucial step in moving past the hoe phase. Casual encounters may have temporarily sated one's physical needs, but they rarely create the meaningful connection to another person that so many people want. To make the transition toward marriage, one must value emotional intimacy and be prepared to put time and effort into developing a stronger relationship with their partner.

Communicating openly and honestly with your partner is crucial if you want to develop emotional connection. Say what you're thinking, hoping, and afraid of. Have in-depth talks that bring you closer together and help you learn more about one another. Intimacy on an emotional level is essential for a relationship to last, yet it is hard to achieve.

Changing relationship styles calls for a greater emphasis on mutual respect and shared ideals in addition to emotional connection. The hoe phase is characterized by a concentration on self-gratification and short-term gratification. But in long-term relationships, you need to take into account your partner's interests and requirements as well as your own.

Check to see if your values coincide with your prospective partner's. Find someone with whom you share values, aspirations, and a way of life. Although diversity of thought and perspective can strengthen a bond, it's vital that partners share core beliefs and ideals.

It is to be expected to face difficulties and setbacks while you make this move. Moving beyond the comfort of informal interactions sometimes brings with it worry and uncertainty. It takes bravery and willingness to go forward into this next period of your life, but remember that change is an integral element of development.

This is a time when introspection is more crucial than ever. Learn to recognize your own limits and requirements, and be honest about them with your partner. Understand that it is important to be patient and empathetic when dealing with relationship challenges.

Changing from the hoe phase to other types of relationships requires a similar shedding of habits and routines that are no longer productive. Don't be afraid to push yourself out of your comfort zone and try something brand new when it comes to interacting with other people. In order to achieve your ideal relationship dynamic, you may need to take steps like establishing boundaries, learning self-discipline, and making deliberate choices.

Finally, keep in mind that committing to another person isn't the final step in the transition process. Maintaining, expanding, and adjusting one's relationships takes work. The road to a lasting commitment can be rocky, but the rewards of a rich emotional connection are well worth the effort.

As we reach the end of this chapter, keep in mind that everyone's path out of the hhomephase and into more

satisfying relationship patterns is distinct. Think about
what you really want, work on growing closer
emotionally, affirm your common beliefs, and be flexible.
Wishing you joy, success, and a bond that lasts far beyond
the hhomephase as you enter this new and exciting chapter
in your lives.

Chapter 13
Learning from Experience: Exposing Personal Stories

In this section, we dig into the anecdotes and experiences of those who have survived the "hoe phase." In addition to entertaining and instructive narratives, readers can learn from the successes and failures of persons who have experienced casual sexual encounters and relationships.

Finding one's way across the exciting yet difficult terrain of casual sex and relationships. Self-discovery, boundary-setting, and gaining insight into one's own wants and needs are common components of this kind of journey. The contributors to this chapter have openly discussed their successes, failures, and everything in between, in the interest of helping others learn from their own experiences.

Sarah, a young woman who got sucked into the hoe phase during her time at university, shares her experience. She opens out about the thrill and introspection of coming to terms with her sexuality. She considers the toll it took on her emotionally and realizes that passing acquaintances left her feeling hollow and dissatisfied. Readers can take away valuable lessons from her experience, including the significance of valuing oneself and being prepared for the emotional fallout of even the most chance of meetings.

Mark's story, however, goes in a different direction. After a long-term relationship ended, he discusses his experience of consciously transitioning into the hoe phase.

It helped him mend wounds and restore his faith in himself. Mark found that spontaneous interactions made him feel liberated and strong. His experiences provide insight into the theory that the hoe phase has varying aeffectson people according to their emotional nneedsand life situations.

Emily's experience sheds light on the tension between pursuing meaningful friendships and engaging in casual sex. She discusses the balancing act of satisfying both physical needs and emotional ties. The lessons of openness, honesty, and self-awareness that she learned via her experiences can be applied to everyday interactions.

The difficulties of the hhomephase are brought home by these individual accounts. They are useful reminders that there is no universal rulebook for sexual intimacy. Every person's path differs since it is molded by their specific experiences, goals, and development.

Our hope is that by reading these accounts, readers will find a wide range of relatable experiences and viewpoints. The purpose of this chapter is to reassure readers that they are not alone in their investigations into casual sexual encounters and relationships. To find the way that is in harmony with our own values, desires, and emotional well-being, we can learn from the experiences of others, both their achievements and their failures.

While reading these accounts, think about how your own life has informed your perspective of the hhomephase. The second half of this chapter will look into the insights and significant takeaways that may be gleaned from these personal anecdotes about casual sex and relationships.

The more we dive into the lives of those who have made it through the dreaded "hoe phase," the more we find that can be applied to our own situations. These anecdotes not only give readers something to relate to, but also illuminate the subtleties and complexities of casual sexuality and relationships from a variety of viewpoints.

Alex, a non-binary person, provides a particularly illuminating account by recounting their experience of the hoe phase from the perspective of gender identity and sexual flexibility. They talk openly about how accepting their gender- and sexuality-ambiguous identities gave them the freedom to experiment with both. Alex's experience illustrates how crucial it is to be one's own person during the hhoephase and to resist the pressure to conform to societal expectations.

Miguel's account, in which he discusses his own attachment styles in the context of chance meetings, is also quite helpful. The author discusses how his neurotic attachment style drove him to look for love and acceptance in casual sexual encounters, only to be left feeling empty and unsatisfied. By engaging in introspection and psychotherapy,

Miguel learned the hard way that he needed to prioritize his own emotional needs and research different attachment styles before getting into casual relationships. His experiences highlight the value of knowing oneself and maintaining one's emotional health when dealing with the nuances of casual sexual encounters and romantic partnerships.

Jade, a woman who used the hoe phase to reclaim her sexuality and challenge conventional gender stereotypes, adds her voice to these experiences. Readers will be encouraged to accept their own impulses and defy conventional expectations after learning about the double standards in Jade's story regarding casual sex. Her experience shows how valuable the hoe phase can be for personal growth and independence.

Bradley, a gay man, concludes by enlightening us on his journey through the hoe phase in the gay, lesbian, bisexual, transgender, and queer community. Bradley discusses the difficulties and discrimination that LGBT people confront, calling for the establishment of safe spaces for sexual experimentation and the promotion of open and frank communication within such settings. His experiences highlight the complexities that gay people must take into account when engaging in casual sex and relationships.

Our hope is that these varied and approachable anecdotes can enrich the exploration of casual sex and relationships among readers. Every person's journey through the hoe phase is different and is shaped by a wide range of circumstances, including but not limited to their gender identity, attachment style, cultural norms, and so on.

It is important to think about how our own life experiences and perspectives about casual sex and relationships have developed as we reflect on these tales. The insights gained from these narratives are priceless. They instruct us on the value of introspection, boundaries, self-awareness, open dialogue, and emotional stability in everyday interactions.

In summary, this chapter's latter half continues to reveal the truths behind the hoe phase through personal anecdotes that are both relevant and instructive. These accounts reassure us that there is no one right way to handle the complexities of casual sex and relationships. When we open ourselves up to and gain wisdom from the experiences of others, we are better able to make decisions that are in line with our values, desires, and psychological health.

Chapter 14

Criticisms and Controversies: Addressing the Community Discourse

Discuss the hoe phase critically, answering frequent objections and addressing disagreements.

The term "hoe phase" has gained popularity in recent years to describe a time in a person's life when he or she has only occasional sexual partners. It's a time of independence and discovery, when people are open about their sexuality and don't look for long-term partnerships. This idea, however, is not without its share of detractors and debaters. We hope to delve into these debates and present a thorough analysis of the hoe phase in this chapter.

The morality concern is often brought up in discussions about the hoe phase's detractors. Promiscuity is generally seen as unethical or immoral because of societal standards and expectations around sexual activity. But it's important to keep in mind that morality is culturally and personally embedded. What one person considers unethical, another may find emancipatory and liberating. We may challenge these ideas and learn about other points of view on sexuality and relationships if we have critical conversations about them.

When discussing the hoe phase, the possibility of emotional injury is another contentious issue. Some worry that having a lot of one-night stands may make people emotionally distant and less able to commit to long-term relationships.

While it's reasonable to be concerned, it's also crucial to remember that the impact on an individual's psyche will differ considerably. Casual interactions can be enriching and empowering for some people and difficult for others. Consent and open dialogue should be given top priority to ensure that everyone is on the same page and knows what is expected of them.

Dismantling the double standards that crop up in community discussions on the hoe phase is also important. Women who openly express their sexuality face more scrutiny and shame from society than their male counterparts. This double standard encourages prejudice and generalizes about women that aren't true. With increased conversation and the elimination of prejudice, we can make the world a safer place for people of all genders to experiment with their sexuality without fear of reprisal.

Discussions of the hoe phase should also take into account the importance of intersectionality. Individuals' perspectives on and engagement with casual sexual encounters are shaped by their unique cultural contexts, life histories, and identities. Sensitivity and an awareness of these divergent viewpoints are necessary for critical discourse. Raising the volume on people of all races, genders, sexual orientations, and socioeconomic backgrounds helps to promote a conversation that welcomes all perspectives.

As we investigate and respond to these concerns and debates over the hoe phase, it's important to keep in mind that there is no silver bullet. It's important to remember that one person's tried-and-true methods might not work for another.

The purpose of this chapter is not to advocate for or against the hoe phase, but to foster communication, tolerance, and insight. By questioning accepted wisdom, busting myths, and encouraging new ways of thinking, we can foster a more inclusive society.

In this chapter's second half, we'll investigate the hoe phase from a psychological and social perspective, looking at how it affects both people and society as a whole. In the next section, we'll take a closer look at the pros and cons of this time of self-discovery and expansion of horizons. Don't close your mind as we learn more about this fascinating subject.In this chapter's second half, we'll investigate the hoe phase from a psychological and social perspective, looking at how it affects both people and society as a whole. Acquiring this knowledge will allow for a more sophisticated understanding of casual sexual encounters and partnerships. So, let's take a closer look at the upsides and downs of this time of discovery and discovery of oneself.

The effect of the hoe phase on one's sense of self-worth and development is an interesting topic to investigate. For some people, having casual sexual partners is a liberating way to test out their sexual boundaries, interests, and preferences. One's sense of control over one's own life, including one's physical self, can grow as a result. And the hoe phase can be a time to figure out what you want out of a long-term relationship and what you can teach your partner about yourself and your emotional needs.

The emotional and mental obstacles that may arise during the hoe phase should not be overlooked, though. Some people experience emotions of vulnerability or loneliness after participating in casual sex. This could be especially true in interactions where there is a lack of understanding, appreciation, and caring. It's crucial to stress the importance of putting one's mental and physical health first in any sexual engagement.

The hoe phase is highly influenced by the individual's sociocultural context. The double standards and stigma that accompany casual sex are sometimes fueled by traditional gender roles and cultural expectations. Particularly harsh criticism and scrutiny is directed at women who openly express their sexuality. The first step in making the world a better place for everyone involves breaking away from these standards and defying societal expectations.

Furthermore, the hoe phase cannot be discussed without addressing the intersections of race, gender, sexuality, and socioeconomic status. Casual sexual encounters may be viewed and experienced differently depending on one's community and cultural background. Intersectionality emphasizes the need for safe and welcoming environments where people from all walks of life can communicate openly and comfortably. A more engaging and powerful discussion on the hoe phase can be fostered through the amplification of diverse viewpoints and the promotion of dialogue.

It's also crucial to remember that not everyone progresses through the hoe phase in the same way. Different people are at different points in their lives, and casual sex may represent a permanent choice for some while being a transitory experiment for others. It doesn't matter how long it lasts, it's always important to respect other people's decisions. In conclusion, engaging in casual sexual encounters is indicative of the hoe phase, which is a time of exploration and self-discovery.

A more complete understanding of the issue can be attained by exploring its psychological and social contexts in greater depth. To promote open discourse, combat prejudices, and provide a more welcoming and inclusive atmosphere for all persons to explore their sexuality, it is important to understand the possible benefits, emotional obstacles, and sociocultural effects surrounding the hoe phase. Don't close your head while we explore more of this intriguing issue; instead, have an open mind and remember that everyone's experiences and perspectives are valid.

Chapter 15
Embracing Individuality: Empowering Personal Choices

When it comes to sexuality and relationships, it can be extremely difficult to be yourself in a world that constantly pushes us to fit in. We are subject to the unyielding standards of our society, which tell us exactly what we can and cannot do. But it's important to remember that everyone's path through these areas of life is different, and that everyone has their own tastes.

We can't expect everyone to have the same level of comfort with casual sex and relationships, and that's okay. It's acceptable that what helps one individual may not help another. Numerous influences, including upbringing, personal ideals, and life experiences, determine our experiences, wants, and boundaries. Recognizing our uniqueness is essential, as is the freedom to make decisions that seem right for us as individuals.

There may be social stigmas linked to casual sex, particularly for women. Many people look down on the concept of going through a "hoe phase" or openly experimenting with one's sexuality. But now is the time to speak out and dispel these myths for good. Casual, consensual sexual activity does not diminish our value as human beings or our right to be loved and respected. It's a free will decision that can lead to new experiences, insights, and deeper connections with others and with oneself.

It takes introspection and self-awareness to chart one's own course through the maze of casual sex and relationships. Establishing, sharing, and enforcing mutually acceptable boundaries between all parties involved is crucial. By accepting and celebrating our uniqueness, we give ourselves permission to act in ways that are true to our values and principles, regardless of what others may think.

It is crucial to communicate openly and honestly while on this path of self-discovery. Casual sexual encounters may not necessarily lead to a committed relationship, but that does not mean there are no feelings involved. Navigating possible difficulties and avoiding misunderstandings can be aided by setting clear expectations and understanding the objectives of both parties involved. Regardless of the type of relationship, everyone has the right to have their needs and feelings taken into account.

Accepting one's uniqueness entails recognizing the wide variety of sexual and romantic encounters that exist. It's important to remember that not everyone will benefit from the same approaches. There's room for casual hookups, committed relationships, platonic friendships, and everything in between. By recognizing and honoring this variety, we can foster a community that welcomes everybody without prejudice or discrimination.

Self-discovery is something that never ends, so keep that in mind as we move forward on this path of celebrating uniqueness and fostering agency. Though our present circumstances and decisions may alter who we become in the future, they do not completely determine who we will be. What's most important is being honest with ourselves and regularly reevaluating our wants and needs, regardless of whether we choose to engage in casual sex or pursue more traditional partnerships.

By discussing casual sexual encounters and relationships, we encourage others to be themselves and take control of their own lives. Let us enjoy our differences and similarities and help one another along the way as we negotiate this complex terrain.

A relationship built on mutual consent, open lines of communication, and respect stands on firm ground. These considerations take on an even greater importance when having casual sex. Both people should be very honest about what they want and where they draw the line before starting anything sexual. Consensual experiences can then take place in an atmosphere where everyone is on the same page.

It's also crucial to approach these conversations with compassion and sensitivity to the feelings and frailties of those with whom we interact. Understanding that feelings and desires can exist beyond the bounds of a committed relationship is what casual sex entails, not emotional detachment or contempt for one another's feelings. When we create a safe place for honest expression, we give ourselves and our partners the freedom to feel and express whatever is going on inside.

It's vital to remember that mistakes and misconceptions are possible as we continue our investigation into casual sex. Because we are human, relationships might have subtleties that can be difficult to decipher. It's important to have empathy and a willingness to talk things out when disagreements or confrontations emerge. By overcoming these issues, we foster a setting conducive to introspection and development.

The social judgments and stigmas that may surround casual sex are something we must face head-on as we embrace our unique selves. In reality, regardless of social norms, everyone has the freedom to act in accordance with their own ideals and goals. Consensual casual sex, whether it occurs during a "hoe phase" or at any other time in our lives, should not be looked down upon or judged negatively.

This allows us to take back control of our own stories. We refuse to accept the premise that our value rests on conforming to outdated, patriarchal standards. Instead, we value the fact that we are all different and have come to different conclusions about life because of it.

In this chapter, we have discussed the significance of valuing one's unique qualities, engaging in casual sex and relationships with integrity, and questioning commonly held beliefs. As we wrap up, keep in mind that learning about oneself is a continuing process. Since our wants and needs can change over time, it's important to do self-checks on a frequent basis to make sure we're being genuine.

 Let us rejoice in the many different kinds of casual sexual encounters and partnerships. Doing so helps to create a space where people can express themselves without fear of reprisal. Let's keep shattering the norms and inspiring one another to be themselves and take charge of their lives.

In this complex setting, let's be there for each other by celebrating our differences and acknowledging our similarities. May we create a world where casual sex and relationships are handled with kindness, respect, and understanding, allowing each of us to have authentic, satisfying relationships.